IMAGES OF ENGLAND

SELLY OAK
AND SELLY PARK

THE OLD OAK
SELLY OAK

IMAGES OF ENGLAND

SELLY OAK
AND SELLY PARK

JOANNE BUTLER, ANNE BAKER
AND PAT SOUTHWORTH

TEMPUS

Frontispiece: The oak tree at the junction of Bristol Road and Oak Tree Lane, 1908.

First published 2005

Tempus Publishing Limited
The Mill, Brimscombe Port,
Stroud, Gloucestershire, GL5 2QG
www.tempus-publishing.com

British Library Cataloguing in Publication Data.
A catalogue record for this book is available from the British Library.

ISBN 0 7524 3625 2

Typesetting and origination by Tempus Publishing Limited.
Printed in Great Britain.

Contents

Acknowledgements

First, we express our gratitude to David Buxton of Tempus for giving us the opportunity to publish this book and guiding us through.

Many of the photographs are from collections in the Local Studies and History section and the Archives of the Birmingham Central Reference Library. Our thanks are due to the staff of the library, in particular to Patrick Baird, Alison Smith and Brian Gambles (Head of Central Library) for helping to make the photographs available. We owe a huge debt of thanks to Tom Hill who generously made available his priceless collection of old postcards. We would also like to express our gratitude to Geoff Dowling who provided photographs collected for *Selly Oak Past and Present* which he co-authored (page 11 above, 12 below, 19a, 19b, 30, 36b, 37a, 67a, 67b, 68a, 93b, 109b) and to Andrew Maxam, particularly for the use of his postcards of public houses (56a, 75b, 85a, 86a, 101a, 102a, 103a, 103b, 104a, 105a). We also thank the staff of Selly Oak Library and Stirchley Library for letting us use the photographs in their local history collections.

We are also very grateful to the following who loaned us images: Barry Toon (112a, 112b); Birmingham University Staff Housing Association (16b, 17a, 62b); Carl Chinn (50b, 65a, 65b, 66a, 89b); Chris Upton (60a); Convent of the Sisters of Charity of St Paul, Selly Park (14a); Tom and Daisy Richards (83a, 83b, 90a); Ecce Scott (16a, 17b); Eileen Hawkins (35a, 35b); Elsie Faulkner (82b, 126a); the family of George Cooper (17b); F.E. Bell (108b); Hilda Lucas (111b); James Wright (78b); Margery Przywala (77b); Jeanne Glenn (68b, 69, 110a, 111a); John Gale (61a, 61b); Lesley Tilley (60b); Linda Chew (116a); Mary Harding (89a); Phil Smallbone (55, 70b); Rhodia Consumer Specialities Ltd (29a & b); Roger Booth, Boxfoldia (38, 39a); Selly Oak Nursery (80a, 81a); Selly Park Property Owners' Association (80b); Shirley Elsden (63b); Simmons Aerofilms Ltd (34a); St Mary's Church, Selly Oak (18, 74b); St Stephen's Church, especially Margaret Twiss (76a, 77a, 77b, 79a, 79b, 121a). Adam Lloyd helped us scan a number of pictures. James Goad provided us with information on the lime kilns.

Last but not least, we would like to thank our families and long-suffering husbands (Ian Butler, John Snell and Henry Southworth) for supporting and helping us with this project. In particular, John Snell exercised his photographic skills on our behalf and Henry Southworth proofread the initial draft. Without their help this book could not have been written. So many people helped us in different ways, we fear we may have omitted to mention someone. In this case, please forgive our lapse and accept our sincere apologies.

Introduction

'Selly' occurs in the Domesday Book (1086) but there is evidence of earlier human occupation. Small pieces of prehistoric, probably Iron Age, pottery and a piece of worked flint were found on the Selly Park (Raddlebarn) Recreation Ground in 1996 which may indicate the site of an Iron Age farmstead in the vicinity. The area also lay close to the Roman fort at Metchley. Ricknield Street, from Alcester to the Roman site at Wall, follows the line of the Pershore Road in Stirchley. Although there is no trace of the road through Selly Oak or Selly Park, a spindle whorl dating to the Roman period was found on the Selly Park Recreation Ground and several Roman coins have been found locally. The well-drained sand and gravel plateau on which the Recreation Ground stands was probably farmed in the Anglo-Saxon era. The name 'Selly' means 'a clearing on a shelf of land' and there is a distinct plateau starting at the Recreation Ground and running to the edge of the manor near Woodbrook. The Domesday survey tells us that there were two manors here, belonging to Tumi and Eleva. The boundaries of these very early estates are unknown but probably included the waterways with Anglo-Saxon names – the Bourn Brook and the River Rea. By 1086 Selly was a sub-manor of the large manor of Northfield whose lord was the Norman baron, William Fitz Ansculf, who was also lord of Dudley Castle. Selly was a small part of Northfield with only seven households in 1086.

The records of the medieval manor court tell us that there was a 'Mill Lane' (Dogpool Lane?) and Hall Lane 'overhung with branches' (Bournbrook Road?). There is a reference to 'Selly Hall' (location uncertain) and to a 'mulle grene' (mill green). Old field names such as 'Lower Bendy' and 'Over Bendy' hint at a landscape of medieval open field agriculture. It is possible that Dogpool Mill on the River Rea was the manorial mill. There was also a mill on the Bourn Brook near the modern-day Grange Road, where recent archaeological investigation has shown that the mill leats are medieval in origin. The medieval settlement at Selly was not grouped round a village green but scattered across the manor, typical of settlements in north Worcestershire. There is no record of a church or a chapel here – the inhabitants of Selly would have walked to their parish church at Northfield. The area now occupied by the Selly Park Recreation Ground is possibly the site of a medieval hunting park.

The heart of medieval Selly lay in its northern part, around Selly Park and Bournbrook Road. However, from the mid-eighteenth century the name 'Selly' is gradually replaced in the records by 'Selly Oak' (first reference 1746). Initially usage seems to refer only to the Bristol Road and Oaktree Lane/Harborne Lane crossing. The name change probably coincides with the turnpiking of the Bristol Road in the early eighteenth century, which was followed later in that century by the construction of the Worcester & Birmingham Canal, which opened as far as Selly Oak by 1795 and by 1815 had been joined at Selly Oak by the Dudley Canal (No. 2 Line), creating a significant canal basin. Several wharves were built to handle coal, lime and bricks. Recent investigation following the closure of Goodman's builders' yard has revealed the existence of several lime kilns. One of the first factories attracted here was Sturge's, making citric acid and later phosphorus for matches (1833). Others followed later, such as Elliott's Patent Sheathing and Metal Company (1855), the Birmingham Battery Company (1871), the Patent Enamel Company (1889), Ariel motorcycles (1890s), the gunmakers Westley Richards (1900) and Ward's Engineering (c. 1914). The 1870s also saw the arrival of the first trams on the Bristol Road and in 1876 the Birmingham West Suburban Railway was opened. The railway and the canal became, in effect, the boundary between Bournbrook and Selly Oak, further concentrating development towards Selly Oak. By the late nineteenth century the whole of the former 'Selly' area had become 'Selly Oak' and in 1911 it officially became a suburb of Birmingham.

The nineteenth century saw the gradual disappearance of the farms under the pressure of increasing industrialisation and the demand for building land. In 1840 there were seven farms in 'Selly Yield' (Selly Hall Farm, Selly Farm, Dog Pool Farm, Five Gates Farm, Raddlebarn Farm, Langley's Farm and Bournbrook Farm). These were mainly given over to pasture with meadow along the river valleys and, apart from the 200-acre farm of Selly Hall, most were less than 50 acres. Some were converted into 'gentlemen's residences' such as Selly Hill Farm on Bournbrook Road and Langley's Farm, which simply became 'The Langleys' after 1840.

The area was always attractive for those wanting a rural retreat. Kirby's Pools in Bournbrook offered an exciting day out and for those who wanted a more permanent semi-rural life (and who had profited from the expanding industry and commerce) there were several minor country houses (Selly Hall, Selly Wick House, Selly Oak House, Selly Hill House and Selly Grove). Of these, only Selly Hall and Selly Wick House remain. Selly Park developed as a spacious residential district in a similar way to neighbouring Edgbaston. Restrictive covenants produced an area of low-density housing, attracting the professional middle classes, who were able to live in the country and work in the town.

From the 1870s, roads of speculative housing began to appear as farmland came on the market. The two estates Heeley/Hubert/Dawlish/Tiverton Roads and Lottie/Winnie/Lottie/Gleave Roads were built mainly between 1870 and 1900. The Grange/North Road estate was built soon after. In the early years of the twentieth century houses were built on the land between the Pershore Road and the River Rea to cater for the increasing number of lower middle classes who were moving out to the suburbs. The Corisande/Durley Dean Road estate was built on farmland from the 1930s.

From the mid-twentieth century onwards, as the older industries declined and were not replaced, the impact of an expanding University of Birmingham has been felt increasingly. The demography of the area has radically changed as many of the houses built for the better-off working class have been occupied by university students. A suburban High Street which once catered for all ages is now almost exclusively geared to the eighteen to twenty-one age bracket.

The twenty-first century will bring further changes. The building of a new hospital, combining the site of the former Selly Oak Hospital and the Queen Elizabeth Hospital, will significantly affect the local road network. Part of this new network will be constructed across land left derelict after the departure of major industry. There are plans to reopen a section of the Dudley Canal and to recreate the canal basin for tourists, not industrial purposes. The High Street in Bournbrook and Selly Oak may no longer need to be an impersonal dual carriageway, but with some imaginative planning, could again be an attractive suburban street.

one

The rural
past

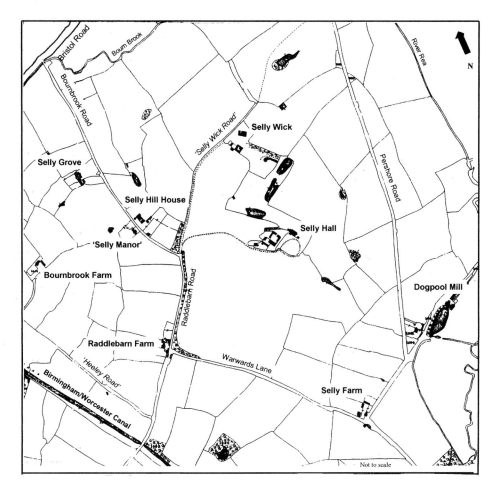

Part of the tithe map of 1840 indicating the rural nature of this part of the Selly area. Some of the farms and principal residences are shown. With the exception of the 200-acre farm attached to Selly Hall, the farms were fairly small. The later 'Heeley Road' and 'Selly Wick Road' were, in 1840, just tracks leading to Bournbrook Farm and Selly Wick House respectively. The medieval road pattern of Warwards Lane, Raddlebarn Road and Bournbrook Road can clearly be seen. The Pershore Road was less than twenty years old when this map was drawn – its newness can be seen in the way it cuts across field boundaries.

Opposite above: The Bourn Brook, *c.* 1915. This section of the Bourn Brook is near Harborne reservoir. The brook rises near Quinton and flows into the River Rea in Cannon Hill Park. It forms part of an ancient boundary – the northern boundary of the manor of Selly and probably of the Anglo-Saxon kingdom of the Hwicce.

Opposite below: Selly Oak, 1925. Harborne Lane, before it was widened, is on the left. The Bourn Brook is in the middle foreground with the bridge just visible on the left, and Harborne Mill beyond. Metchley Lane can just be identified in the far distance with the public house the Golden Cross at the base of the lane. There are allotments in the shallow valley of the Bourn Brook. A horse grazes in the field. This tranquil scene was to change radically within only a few years.

AT HARBORNE RD. RESERVOIR SELLY OAK

Front view of Raddlebarn Farm, in 1963, which stood on Raddlebarn Road at its junction with
Warwards Lane (from where this photograph is taken). The farm was known as 'Raddle Barn
Doors Farm' in the earliest reference in 1776 and for some time afterwards. It was a farm of 50
acres, mainly used for grazing cattle. The name may derive from 'Reddle' – the dye used to mark
sheep, or 'Rattle' – referring to the noise of the barn doors on a windy day!

This view of Raddlebarn Road (postmarked 1909) was taken looking east towards the junction
with Tiverton Road. Raddlebarn Farm can be seen, as well as the barn with its large doors from
which the name may derive. Although the upper sections of Dawlish, Tiverton and Hubert Roads
and Teignmouth Road were built across its fields between 1898 and 1910, the farmhouse survived
until 1974 when it was demolished and a row of modern terraced housing built. The cowshed
remained until the 1990s and was in use for a while as a fabric shop.

Selly Farm, 1960. This farm stood at the junction of Warwards Lane and St Stephen's/School Road. The earliest reference to it is in 1809. Before the Pershore Road was constructed in 1825 this was a significant road junction leading from Selly (Oak) to Kings Heath. Selly Farm was a mixed farm of about 96 acres and was occupied for several decades in the nineteenth century by the Warwood family, from whom the name 'Warwards Lane' may originate.

Selly Farm, at an unknown date. This view of Selly Farm is taken from Warwards Lane, looking towards the Pershore Road. Surrounded by houses, the farmhouse is now for sale. Milner, Westminster, Umberslade and Gristhorpe Roads were built across its fields around 1904. The farmhouse was demolished in the 1970s to be replaced by a petrol station and then by an apartment block.

Left: Selly Hall, *c.* 1830. This is the earliest known photograph of Selly Hall, a Grade II-listed building, now part of the Roman Catholic Convent of the Order of the Sisters of Charity of St Paul, on Selly Park Road in Selly Park. A hall at Selly is first mentioned in 1428, possibly a predecessor of this building, which is of mid- to late eighteenth-century date. The architect was one of the Wyatt family of architects. Selly Hall had a large estate (approximately 200 acres) which covered most of modern-day Selly Park.

Below: Selly Hall, at an unknown date. The Hall was bought by the Roman Catholic order in 1864. They added wings to the original house, as well as building an enclosing wall with a gatehouse. Further buildings were added later, including the cloisters (1880s), the administration block (1900), the chapel (1915) and an infirmary in 1932.

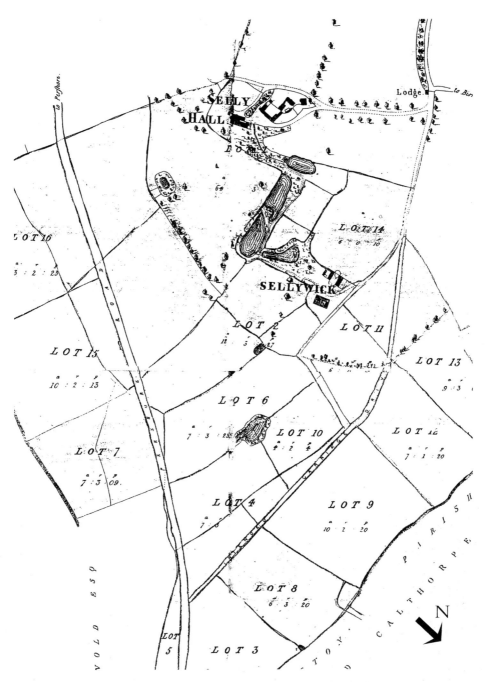

Sale plan of the Selly Hall estate, 1835. This is the map which accompanied the sale of Selly Hall in 1835, when it was bought by a Birmingham lawyer, Robert Dolphin, who paid £25,000 for the Hall, Selly Wick and '200 acres of fine turf land'. Selly Hall Farm is visible (as a rectangular block) in front of the Hall, at the end of the carriage drive leading to the top of Bournbrook Road, roughly the line of present-day Selly Avenue. Note the lakes which linked Selly Hall to Selly Wick. The Pershore Road was only ten years old when this map was drawn. The 'intended carriage drive' follows a similar line to modern-day Upland Road.

A modern view of Selly Wick House, a Grade II-listed building on Selly Wick Road. It was probably built in the 1780s and was described in 1835 as an 'excellent residence ... a family house ... with carriage house, stables, outoffices, gardens, plantations, fish stews and several pieces of rich pasture land'. The Ryland and Pinsent families were connected with the house for many years until they sold it in 1949 to the University of Birmingham. Selly Wick House is now used for offices.

The lake in the grounds of Selly Wick House, c. 1967. One of a series of lakes on the Selly Hall estate. A boathouse is visible on the far side of the lake. The lake was drained in the late 1960s and the filled-in lake, known as 'The Dell', was a favourite play area for children from the university staff housing estate. The land was sold in 1989 and houses built on the site.

Selly Wick Cottage, 1987. This cottage was in the grounds of Selly Wick House. Initially it was the cottage for the groom to the family living at the house. From 1891 onwards it became known as the 'gardener's cottage'. It was demolished when the land was sold for houses.

The family of the gardener, c. 1901. In 1891 the gardener's cottage was occupied by George Cooper and his family. This picture of the family, with George Cooper seated in the middle with some of his seven children and their husbands/wives, was taken in the courtyard at the back of Selly Wick Cottage. From the 1950s to 1985 the cottage was occupied by Annie and Ted Shemilt who previously had been in service to the Pinsent family.

SELLY·OAK·HOUSE
in 1846.

Selly Oak House, pictured here in 1846, stood near Oak Tree Lane and was originally a substantial farmhouse, converted into a 'gentleman's residence' by local auctioneer John Rodway who bought it in 1825. John Rodway has been incorrectly attributed with planting the oak from which the name Selly Oak is derived. The grounds of Selly Oak House were sold in 1875 to a developer, John Abraham, who developed Katie, Winnie, Lottie and Gleave Roads on the site (named after the children of Henry Elliott of Elliott's Metal Company). Selly Oak House itself was demolished soon after and no trace remains of the mini country estate created here by John Rodway, with its impressive carriage drive, pools, fishponds, orchards, lawns and a formal garden.

Opposite, above: A side view of Selly Manor in 1907. Part of Selly Hill House is visible in the background. The picture was taken from 'Rookery Footpath,' an old footpath (possibly a medieval lane), which ran alongside the cottages to Bournbrook Farm and then to Harborne, via Selly Oak. It was a very popular country walk but was closed in 1906, despite a vigorous local campaign to keep it. As the only buildings of any antiquity in the area, there have been many tales associated with the cottages. It is claimed that Richard III slept here on his way to the battle of Bosworth Field.

Opposite, below: Selly Manor, *c.* 1900? At the time of the photograph this building was, in fact, three cottages, known as 'Rookery Cottages' or 'The Rookeries' (hence 'Rookery Road'). In the late nineteenth century the steward of the manor of Northfield, Frank Pearson, believed them to be the medieval manor house of Selly, the home for a while of the lords of the manor, the Jouette (more correctly Jonette) family. The cottages were moved at George Cadbury's expense in 1912 and restored as the centre piece of his model village, opening to the public in 1917.

18

The oak in Selly on a postcard dated 1906. This is the old oak tree from which it is believed Selly Oak derives its name. The name 'Selly Oak' first appears in the middle of the eighteenth century when it applied only to a small area where the Bristol Road is crossed by Harborne Lane and a lane now called 'Oak Tree Lane'. The oak stood on the north side of the lane very close to the crossroads. It was romanticised as the site of a witch's burial. Although not on a parish boundary, it was also suggested that the oak was a holy or gospel oak which would have been visited at Rogationtide at the annual beating of the parish boundaries, to ensure their remembrance. It was also claimed by the descendants of a local family, the Rodways, that an ancestor had planted the oak around 1830 to mark a special occasion. However, because the stump was preserved in Selly Oak Park when the tree was felled in 1909, it was possible in 2001 to date the tree by its rings. The results cast doubt on all previous theories. The tree had actually begun growing in the first part of the eighteenth century, just before the first recorded reference to 'Selly Oak'. From 1726 the Bristol Road had been turnpiked, and a toll gate erected at the crossroads in question, necessitating a description of the 'stop' on the turnpike. As a prominent feature, the oak seems to have been used to describe the location, rather as public house names might mark bus stops. From the crossroads the name began to cover a wider area as the area became more populated with the construction of the Worcester & Birmingham Canal.

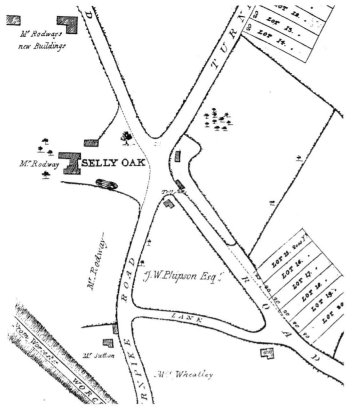

Left: Part of a map of 1829 showing the prominent oak tree. The site where the oak stood had originally been open common land but had been enclosed by John Rodway to create his country estate of Selly Oak House. It was claimed that John Rodway planted the oak in 1830, but as this map of 1829 shows, the oak was already there, along with the name 'Selly Oak'.

Below: The oak, from a postcard marked 1911. The oak became a familiar and much loved part of the landscape and community. Some believed it to be a very ancient tree which had stood on 'the village green', although Selly Oak never actually had a traditional village green. Note the row of terraces behind the tree. These were called 'Selly Oak Place' and at the time of the photograph were still houses with front gardens. They later became shops.

THE OAK TREE, SELLY OAK.

Above: The oak in 1894. The old oak encroached on both the pavement and the road of the rapidly developing suburb. So, in the late nineteenth century, the authorities sought its removal as a dangerous obstruction.

Left: Handbill, *c.* 1894. This handbill was produced in support of the oak and signed by many local residents. The oak was about 150 years old when the campaign was launched for it to be spared.

Left: The oak about to be felled, from a postcard marked 1909. Here the axeman continues his work – having already lopped off the branches of the oak. The occasion was a great spectacle for local residents.

Below: The fallen oak, 1909. The end of a landmark. The timber was disposed of but the stump was taken to the nearby Selly Oak Park.

Right: Plaque in Selly Oak Park. This is the inscription on the stump of the old oak tree, now in Selly Oak Park. It reads 'Butt of old oak tree from which the name of Selly Oak was derived. Removed from Oak Tree Lane, Selly Oak, 1909'.

Below: Selly Oak without the oak (undated). Commemoration is not confined to a plaque on a stump. The side of the Sainsbury's store, sited near the crossroads, has an oak tree depicted in its brickwork on the southern side. Also, a new oak tree was planted in 2000 on the south side of Oak Tree Lane to belatedly replace the one felled in 1909.

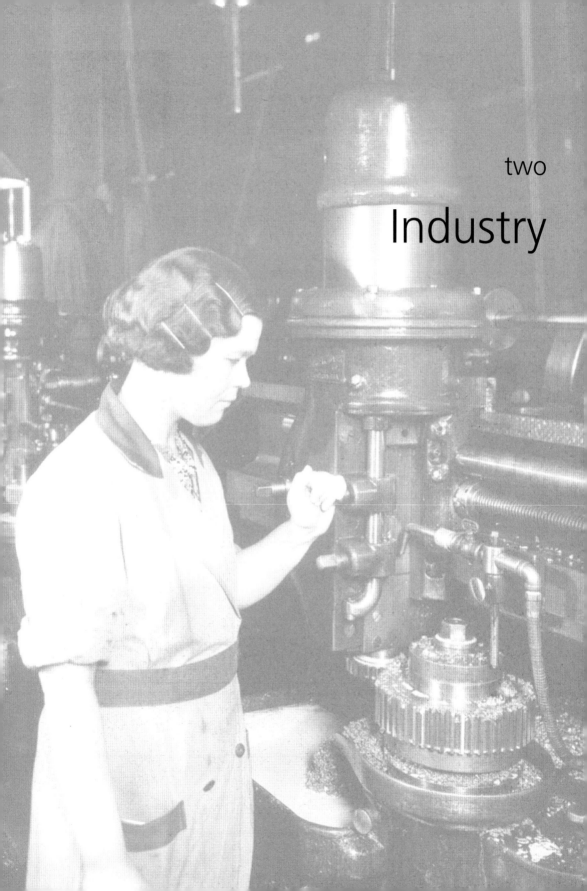

two

Industry

Dogpool Mill buildings and pool photographed around 1950. Dogpool Mill, on the River Rea at Ten Acres, was one of several mills that were situated on the rivers and streams in the Selly Oak area. Many of these mills were originally corn mills, but were later used for industrial purposes. By 1819, Dogpool Mill was producing copper-covered lead pipes as patented by W. Phipson, and John Phipson was the tenant in 1840. It was later occupied by Tomlinson & Co., tube and wire manufacturers, and by 1875 the mill had been taken over by Charles Clifford & Sons, who were metal rollers and tube makers. They were still in occupation as metal manufacturers when this photograph was taken and remained there until the 1980s. During the 1920s and 1930s there were tea rooms and boats for hire at Dogpool Mill pool, and local people fished there.

Opposite above: An aerial view of Dogpool Mill and pool, with Dogpool Lane in the foreground, *c.* 1950.

Opposite below: A similar view of Dogpool Mill at the end of the 1950s after the mill pool had been drained, filled in and buildings constructed on the site.

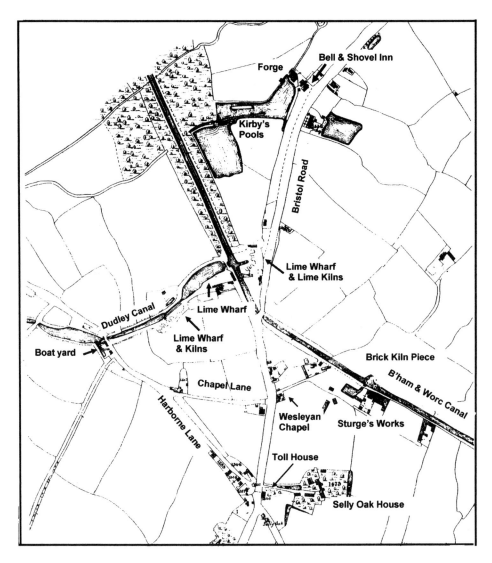

Part of the Northfield tithe map showing Selly Oak in 1840. As the junction at Selly Oak between the Worcester & Birmingham Canal and the Dudley Extension Canal (Dudley No. 2 Canal) was situated alongside the Worcester-Birmingham turnpike road (Bristol Road), these transport links provided an ideal situation for industry to develop. By the early nineteenth century coal and lime wharves had become established around the canal junction. Remains of lime kilns have recently been found here and the wavy lines on this tithe map probably indicate these kilns. Limestone, which could have been transported down the Dudley Canal, was heated with coal to produce lime. This was used in farming to improve the soil, in lime mortar for building, and for various industrial processes.

Within a few years other industrial works were built around this junction, such as the factory of brothers John and Edmund Sturge, who were Quakers and the younger brothers of the philanthropist Joseph Sturge. They had already established works manufacturing chemicals in Wheeleys Lane in Edgbaston and in 1933 they opened the Selly works alongside the Worcester & Birmingham Canal, where initially citric acid was manufactured. This was obtained from concentrated lemon or lime juice and separated by a process that needed lime, so the proximity to the lime kilns was ideal.

This painting of J. & E. Sturge's chemical works in 1844 shows the entry to their canal basin, with a brick arch over it for the towpath. John Sturge died in 1840 and Edmund Sturge took his brother-in-law Arthur Albright into partnership.

LIGHTING EVERY MATCH

A hundred years ago Arthur Albright's idea for making *Amorphous Phosphorus* on a commercial scale brought safety to workers in match factories, and gave the world its first safety match. Today Albright & Wilson's match phosphorus products light every match made in Britain and countless millions of others all over the world.

ALBRIGHT & WILSON LTD

 CHEMICALS

AMORPHOUS PHOSPHORUS · PHOSPHORUS SESQUISULPHIDE

Sturge and Albright decided to produce phosphorus for Lucifer matches at Selly Oak. However, the white form of phosphorus used in these matches is a hazardous material. It readily catches fire when exposed to air and is also very poisonous, making workers liable to develop a disease of the jaw known as 'Phossy Jaw'. By 1849, another form of phosphorus, red phosphorus, had been discovered, which was not poisonous and did not readily catch fire, but it was highly explosive to make. However Albright realised it could be much safer for both workers and users and he developed a process for producing it safely. It was then used for the production of safety matches and an advertisement commemorating this was issued by Albright and Wilson in 1949.

In 1851 phosphorus production was moved to a new factory in Oldbury. The partnership between Edmund Sturge and Arthur Albright was dissolved in 1854 and Albright joined with J.E. Wilson to form Albright & Wilson at Oldbury. Sturge kept the Wheeleys Lane works and later opened a factory further down the canal in Lifford Lane. The Selly works were sold to Elliott's.

Elliott's Metal Co. Ltd as shown in their brochure, *c.* 1910. This company was first incorporated in 1862 to take over the established business of W. Elliott & Sons, Metal Rollers and Wire Drawers, who had bought Sturge's works in 1855. At this time Selly Oak only consisted of a few cottages and so accommodation had to be specially provided for the firm's workers.

In 1866 the business of Charles Green, the inventor and patentee of solid-drawn tubes, was bought and amalgamated into the company. Before this process was invented, brass and copper tubes had seams joined by soldering along their entire length. The works included a refinery, a tube mill for the production of brass and copper tubes, a copper locomotive plate rolling mill and a yellow metal mill. Elliott's was a large manufacturer of yellow metal sheet, which was produced for sheathing the hulls of wooden ships. This was also known as 'Muntz metal', as it had been patented by George Frederick Muntz. Brass and copper wire, aluminium bronze for propeller shafts, and telegraph and trolley bus wires were also manufactured. Elliott's became part of ICI Metals group in 1928 and the factory closed in 1964 when production was transferred to Witton.

Opposite above: This was originally the manager's house for Elliott's factory. After it had become empty in 1891, Henry Elliott, who was concerned about technical education for factory workers, offered it for use as a Technical Institute. Classes continued here until the Technical Institute in Bournbrook was opened in 1899. It is still standing today at the end of Elliott Road, although most of the factory has now been demolished.

Opposite below: An aerial view of the industrial area of Selly Oak near to the canals in 1927/28. The Birmingham Battery & Metal Company factory is in the foreground, with the canal basin on the Dudley Canal visible towards the left-hand side. The chimneys of Elliott's factory can be seen in the background on the other side of the Bristol Road.

Workers at the Birmingham Battery & Metal Company in 1913. This group of men, with both cart-horses and motor vehicles, show that horse-drawn transport was still being used in the works. The company was founded in 1836 under the management of Thomas Gibbins, and their original factory in Digbeth contained rolling mills, and wire and tube mills. Large brass sheets for battery working were also produced. This term arose because, before the development of rolling mills, sheets of metal were made by hammering out a cast ingot of the metal using a 'battery' of hammers of different weights and shapes. By 1836 rolling mills were used to produce flat plates, but items such as bowls, pans and kettles were still produced by power hammering, and these products kept the name of battery.

In 1871 land was bought at Selly Oak alongside the Dudley Canal, a canal basin was constructed and a new factory built. The battery trade had declined and the new premises initially manufactured copper tubes. A copper refinery was then added and the factory gradually expanded with new tube and rolling mills manufacturing products such as seamless copper tubes, brass condenser tubing and parts for locomotives. It became a limited company in 1897 under the directorship of members of the Gibbins family, who also donated land to the council from the Weoley Park estate to form Selly Oak Park.

Opposite above: The north side of the High Street in 1963 showing the Birmingham Battery offices in the background. Although they are now vacant, these offices are due to be retained in the proposed redevelopment of the Battery site. All the other buildings have been demolished.

Opposite below: The hydraulic extrusion plant for making small size copper and copper-alloy tubes was added to the Birmingham Battery works in 1927.

This aerial photograph of 1921 shows the Ariel works in Bournbrook on the industrial area which had been built on the site of Kirby's Pools. Birmingham University is in the background. Ariel motorcycles were first produced around 1900 when Cycle Components Ltd of Bournbrook added a motor to their pedal cycles. Many popular motorcycle models were produced here in the first half of the twentieth century by Ariel Motors Ltd. The company was taken over by BSA (Birmingham Small Arms Co. Ltd) in 1944 and production was moved to Small Heath in 1961.

An Ariel postcard of 1951. In the background are the Dome of Discovery and the Skylon at the 1951 Festival of Britain. It is one of many similar adverts of the period which show fashionable people riding Ariel motorcycles.

Celebrations at Ward's Engineering (H. W. Ward & Co. Ltd) in Dale Road, who began making machine tools in Birmingham in the mid-1890s and moved to Bournbrook around 1914.

Emily Windridge (in the foreground) began working as a gear cutter at Ward's Engineering at the beginning of the Second World War and then remained with the company once the war was over for more than twenty years.

This architects' drawing in 1900 of the new Westley Richards gun factory in Grange Road shows the factory in a rural setting alongside the Bourn Brook with pollarded trees on the opposite bank. Its position allowed a shooting range for trials of the guns to be sited along the stream bank.

Grange Road in 1987 with the Westley Richards factory on the right, largely unchanged, but with an entrance to Birmingham University now on the other side of the brook. The factory on the left was the premises of George Morgan, drop forgers. This building has recently been demolished as the new Selly Oak Relief Road will pass through this site and also that of the Westley Richards factory.

A group of workers from Westley Richards, *c.* 1908. The firm was originally founded by William Westley Richards in High Street, Birmingham, in 1812. The new works in Bournbrook contained a large mill with small workshops for finishing. Quality guns with detailed workmanship are still produced here.

Decimals Ltd were engineers who also had premises in Grange Road. Their wagon was displaying 'Signal and Phosphorous Grenades' and 'Barbed Wire Cutters' as part of Birmingham's 'Win the War' Day on 21 September 1918.

Women workers in the finishing shop at Boxfoldia's Ten Acre Works, *c.* 1930. Boxfoldia moved to the Ten Acre Works on the Pershore Road in Selly Park in 1924, having been founded by Charles Henry Foyle in two rooms in the centre of Birmingham in 1921. They manufactured cartons for well-known companies such as J. & J. Colman, Reckitts and the Dunlop Rubber Company. Foyle believed that business was a partnership between employer and employee, and set up a Works Council, which was unusual at that time. By 1933 these works had become too small and Boxfoldia moved to Dale Road in Bournbrook into premises which were previously part of the Ariel Motors works. Boxfoldia remained in Bournbrook until moving to a new purpose-built carton factory in Redditch around 1990.

Opposite above: Boxfoldia workers outside the rear of their factory in Ten Acres, *c.* 1930.

Opposite below: The Ten Acre Works on the Pershore Road in 1996. Cox, Wilcox & Co. Ltd were domestic hardware manufacturers who had taken over the factory from Boxfoldia in 1934. Only the frontage of the factory now remains.

The Patent Enamel Co. Ltd was formed in 1888 by Benjamin Baugh and William Walters, following the establishment of a successful business in Bradford Street, Birmingham. A new purpose-built factory was opened in 1889 in Heeley Road beside the canal and railway. A canal basin was built, with access to the canal being obtained by tunnelling under the railway embankment. The factory produced tough, decorative vitreous enamel sheets, which were used for advertising on railway stations and in hotels and public houses. After the Second World War demand for these products declined and the factory closed in 1965.

Selly Oak Pumping Station on the Bristol Road photographed in 1973. In the middle of the nineteenth century piped water gradually became available throughout the Birmingham area. The water was obtained from streams and wells and Selly Oak Pumping Station was built in the mid-1870s to take water from a well beneath Selly Oak. When the Elan Valley supply was established in 1904, the pump house was kept in case this should fail, but the well was eventually capped in 1920 and the machinery removed. The building was then used by the Electric Supply Department.

three

Transport

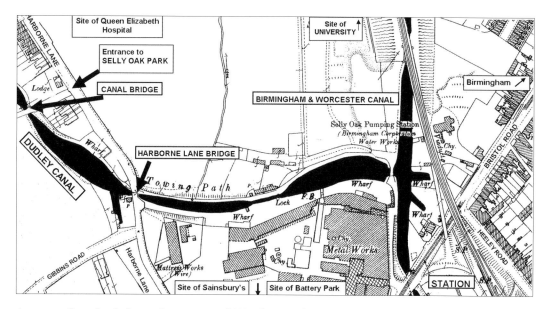

An extract from the Ordnance Survey map of 1884 showing the junction of the Dudley Canal and the Worcester & Birmingham Canal at Selly Oak. The locations of some of the photographs later in the chapter are indicated.

Opposite above: Canal junction, at an unknown date. This rare photograph shows the junction of the Dudley Canal (on the left) with the Worcester & Birmingham Canal, looking towards Birmingham. The Worcester & Birmingham Canal linked Birmingham (at Gas Street Basin) with the River Severn at Diglis Basin. It had been constructed as far as Selly Oak by 1795 and opened along its entire length in 1815 at a cost of £610,000. The canal junction soon attracted industry and the sides were lined with wharves and factories. The Birmingham Battery Company works are on the left and the site of the lime kilns and wharf on the right.

Opposite below: Work on the Dudley Canal, 1929. This photograph is taken from the canal bridge, now a footbridge in Selly Oak Park near its Harborne Lane entrance, looking back towards Selly Oak and the Worcester & Birmingham Canal. The canal bridge in Harborne Lane can be seen in the middle of the picture, as well as the chimneys of the Birmingham Battery Company. Note the distinctive tree on the bridge – see next photograph.

The canal bridge on Harborne Lane, 1922. This is the bridge on Harborne Lane. A coal lorry is passing over the bridge towards Selly Oak. This canal (also known as the Dudley No. 2 or the Netherton Canal) was begun in 1794 to enable coal and lime from Netherton to pass down to the River Severn and, via the Stratford & Avon Canal, down to Oxford and London. A coal wharf was located on this canal in Selly Oak, as well as wharves for bricks and lime on the Worcester & Birmingham Canal.

The canal bridge on Harborne Lane, 1922. The same bridge as the above view from the Selly Oak side. This bridge was part of the main route from Harborne (to the left) to Selly Oak (to the right). The boatyard on the Dudley Canal, set up and run by the Monk family for many years, can be glimpsed under the bridge on the left. The Lapal Tunnel further along the Dudley Canal proved the undoing of this canal – a final roof fall in 1917 led to the closure of the tunnel, cutting off the Selly Oak section.

Drawbridge on Dudley Canal, at an unknown date. The Dudley Canal was cut across fields
and countryside and in Selly Oak required minimal landscaping because it followed the Bourn
Brook Valley. An existing footpath at this point, (near modern-day Corisande Road) required
a drawbridge. The initials on the barge (SND Co.) indicate that it belonged to the Sharpness
New Docks Company, which amalgamated with the Worcester & Birmingham Canal Company
in 1874. This section of canal continued to be used for some years even after the closure of the
Lapal Tunnel, transporting bricks from the brickworks at Stonehouse Farm, Weoley Castle and
California. Smarts Brickworks were the last works to make bricks at California and remained until
the 1950s.

Selly Oak railway station, *c. 1912*. The Birmingham West Suburban Railway line from Granville Street to Kings Norton was opened in 1876 with five stations, including Selly Oak. It was later incorporated into Midland Railway and the terminus changed to New Street. The station staff in this picture are seated in front of the old station buildings, with a railway siding behind the fence. The single track was doubled in the 1880s.

Selly Oak railway station, 1917. This photograph was taken from the station looking across to Heeley Road. In the foreground are a number of wagons belonging to the First Southern and General Military Hospital which was housed in the new Birmingham University buildings. The wagons are waiting for another consignment of war casualties. These convoys often ran at night to avoid noise and traffic.

Old and new bridge, 1958. The railway was carried over the Bristol Road in Selly Oak by an embankment and multi-arched viaduct. In the 1920s the central part of the viaduct was replaced with the present steel bridge to take the new higher trams. The new bridge followed a slightly different alignment, leaving part of the old bridge still *in situ*, seen to the left of the picture. The smaller arches are in use as a timber depot.

The old station (1975). The station complex was rebuilt in 1978 and again in 2003. This view was taken looking towards Birmingham – the Selly Oak Pumping Station can be seen in the distance. The current car park occupies the area that once housed significant goods sidings which could hold up to 300 wagons. The sidings were mainly used for the conveyance of coal and a coal merchant's stood on the site for many years.

Tram shed, 2003. The first trams along the Bristol Road in the 1870s were horse drawn and came only as far as the Bournbrook Hotel (now the Goose at the OVT). Trams initially ran every 15 minutes, with flat fares of 3d for passengers on the inside and 2d for those outside. From 1890 to 1900 the battery, or accumulator, trams ran on the route. With the tram sheds on Dawlish Road, although the access was on Tiverton Road (pictured above). The building was demolished in 2003.

Selly Oak tram depot, 1928. The depot on Chapel Lane was opened in 1927, replacing the depot in Dawlish Road. The new depot could accommodate up to eighty trams. Following the cessation of trams in Birmingham, it was used as a bus depot for many years until it closed in 1986. The building remains and is now in use as a storage centre.

Tram at Chapel Lane, 1952. Here a tram is heading for the depot further down Chapel Lane with another tram following closely behind. The Plough and Harrow pub is on the left. The tramlines had been extended to Chapel Lane in 1900. The weight of the batteries required for the trams led to the abandonment of accumulator trams and the Bristol Road route became the first in Birmingham to be fitted with overhead electric cables in 1901.

Tram on Bristol Road, 1952. A tram entering the central reservation tramway as it leaves Selly Oak. The line was extended as far as Rednal in 1924 and the eight-mile route from Navigation Street was a vital part of a day out at the Lickeys.

Bournbrook tram (undated). One of the many comic cards issued about trams, graphically illustrating some of the dangers of tram travel!

High Street, Bournbrook, 1952. Electric trams ceased to run in Birmingham in 1952 and buses took over the routes. This picture shows the tram lines being pulled up on the Bristol Road in Bournbrook on 22 August 1952. The trams were broken up at the Witton depot but many were stored temporarily on the central reservation of the Bristol Road, prior to their final journey across the city.

Toll-gate on Pershore Road, 1928. This toll-gate and cottage on the Pershore Road were located near Pebble Mill. The Pershore Road was opened in 1825 as a turnpike road. The photograph appears to be taken looking along the Pershore Road towards Selly Park with the chimneys of the Selly Park Tavern in the distance. Trams were introduced in 1904, later than the Bristol Road. As elsewhere in Birmingham, they were discontinued in 1952.

Pershore Road, 1951. The creation of the Pershore Road opened up opportunities for housing and businesses along its route. This substantial Victorian villa became the premises of road haulage companies, first British Road Services, and, from 1953 until 1997, Brookvale Transport. The extensive area of land behind, between the Pershore Road and the River Rea, could accommodate up to 100 lorries. The building remained until 2000 when the site was redeveloped for housing.

Harborne Lane looking towards Harborne, 1926. Harborne Lane was the old road from Selly Oak to Harborne. This photograph is taken just before major widening. On the left is the later entrance to Selly Oak Park. Harborne Mill is at the bottom of the hill, and in the far distance is Metchley Lane.

Harborne Lane, *c.* 1924? This photograph is taken as road widening begins. The old lane runs along the left of the picture, past Harborne Mill and up towards the junction with Metchley Lane. In the days before modern road-making machinery, manpower and horse power sufficed. A pile of pipes lies on the side ready to be laid along the side of the new road. The old narrow bridge over the Bourn Brook can be seen on the left.

The bridge on Harborne Lane, 1924. The finished result – the narrow bridge has been replaced and the road considerably widened. The public house, The Golden Cross, with its white frontage, can be seen at the bottom of Metchley Lane.

Harborne Lane, 1935. Further improvements were made to Harborne Lane by the creation of a dual carriageway. A carriageway was added to the right of the original road – the trees in the central reservation are probably the hedgerows of the old lane. The entrance to Selly Oak Park can be seen on the left and new houses have been built alongside the new carriageway.

Smallbone's gargage, 1939. Harold Smallbone moved from Stirchley to open the garage on the corner of Raddlebarn and Gristhorpe Road in 1929 and the garage has remained in the family since then. In this photograph work is being carried out on an entrance to the yard of the house. The house was lived in by Harold and Eva Smallbone. Both Harold and his son Percy are in the photograph. The vehicle is a Morris Commercial truck.

Opposite above: Raddlebarn Road, 1909. Raddlebarn Road was formerly known as 'Gypsy Lane' and was part of a medieval road pattern, running along the plateau on which the settlement of Selly was first established. This view is looking west with the junction of Warwards Lane (another old lane) to the left and Tiverton Road to the right. The left-hand side is still residential, but even by 1909 the houses on the right hand side had been converted to shops. The corner shop has a sign saying 'Raddlebarn Road Post Office'.

Opposite below: Raddlebarn Road, 1967. By 1967 the post office had moved to this corner. Next to it is the premises of A.E. Parkes, a seedsman. The bold advertising is for Smallbone's garage.

Raddlebarn Road, at an unknown date. The two cyclists are heading towards Bournbrook Road. St Edward's School and Church is on the left and Raddlebarn Recreation Ground, enclosed by railings, is on the right. In the distance is the boundary wall (and the trees) of a large Victorian property known as 'Elmdon' which was demolished in the 1930s and a number of houses built on the plot.

Bournbrook Road, 1911. Originally called 'Hall Lane', this was also part of the medieval road pattern, leading to the Bristol Road and on to Edgbaston and Birmingham. The three-storied houses on the left, as well as the terraces lower down the road, were built in the 1890s. Note the newly built University of Birmingham in the background.

four

Houses and housing estates

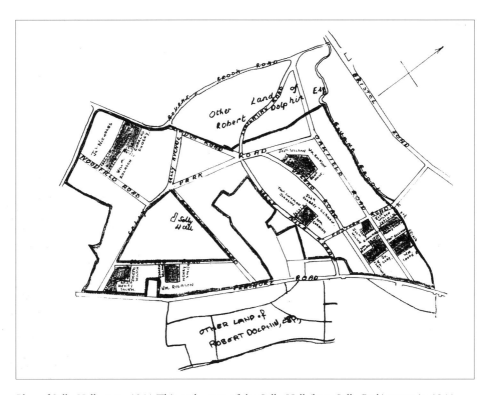

Plan of Selly Hall estate, 1864. This early map of the Selly Hall (later Selly Park) estate in 1864 shows the road layout of the new estate and the building plots, some of which had already been built upon. Selly Hall and its 200-acre estate were bought by Robert Dolphin in 1835, but he lived in the Hall for only a short time, preferring to rent it out. In 1854 he sold 154 acres of the estate, excluding the Hall, to a Land Society (Counties Permanent Building Investment and Land Society). The Society planned the layout of a new estate aimed at the professional middle classes. All the building plots on the estate were subject to a number of conditions or restrictive covenants, which determined how the estate developed. Each plot was to be no less than ¼ acre (many were 1 acre), only detached or semi-detached properties could be built, and a minimum distance set back from the road. These covenants are still in force today and have resulted in the development of a distinctive area of low-density housing.

Opposite above: The Uplands, 1967. This is the bay window of No. 63 Upland Road which was one of a pair of houses built in the 1860s, complete with their own mini country estate – 6 acres of grounds laid out as gardens with ornamental trees, paths, pools and greenhouses. The whole estate was surrounded by a high brick wall, lending an air of exclusivity. The spring-fed pools survive in one of the gardens in Upland Road. In the early 1970s No. 63 was demolished to make way for a block of flats, 'Seymour Close'. No. 65 survives today.

Opposite below: A modern view of the terrace and stables of the Uplands. The two houses originally faced each other across this terrace with stables beneath. For many years the houses were occupied by the Winn and Webley families, related by marriage. They were typical of the early residents on the estate – the Winns were brassfounders and the Webleys were gunmakers. Both had their factories in the town centre. Every Monday morning fresh vegetables were loaded onto the Winn carriage from the Uplands gardens for distribution to the employees at his brass foundry.

Murals from Highfield, photographed in 1984. Highfield was another large Victorian house built in the early 1860s. From 1929 to 1982 it was owned by Professor Sargant Florence, Professor of Economics at the University of Birmingham, and became the centre of an alternative 'Bloomsbury' where artists, writers, left-wing politicians (e.g. W.H. Auden and Bertrand Russell) would meet for discussions. Lella Florence (pictured above) painted extensively, including these frescoes at Highfield. The house was demolished in 1984 and a development of houses built on its 4 acres of grounds, although the lake and some other features were retained.

View from Oakfield Road, pre-1932. This picture was taken from 107 Oakfield Road looking out towards the Bristol Road and Edgbaston. The Bourn Brook runs across allotments in the foreground. By the 1930s these allotments had been built upon.

Baden House, Oakfield Road, at an unknown date. This house was built in 1904 for Mr Harris, a plumber, whose business premises was on the Bristol Road. The Selly Park estate attracted successful trade and professional classes who wanted to emulate the lifestyle of the upper classes. It became possible to maintain a successful business in town while living in a rural/semi-rural environment of one of the new middle-class suburbs such as Selly Park.

The garden of Baden House. The new Selly Park estate was an ideal location – out of town, yet only a carriage ride away, on wooded slopes and upwind of Birmingham's smoke and fumes. Note in this photograph the empty plot to the left, used for keeping a horse. Before the widespread access to the motor car, a horse-drawn carriage was the main means of transport and such vacant plots had their uses. The Selly Park estate developed very gradually, with plots undeveloped into the twentieth century.

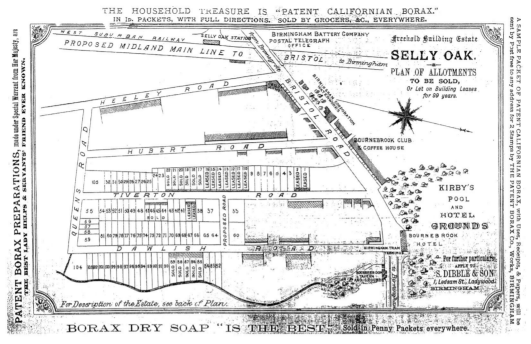

Plan of the Selly Oak building estate 1882. A limited development of roads and building plots specifically for the labouring classes was begun in Selly Oak in the 1870s and an advert, along with this map, was placed to attract more speculators. The accompanying text reads 'the rapidly increasing population of the labouring classes in Selly Oak renders this estate a favourable field for builders and those desirous of acquiring a freehold lot of land'. Cleaner, semi-rural living was attractive to everyone, but for the working classes, without private transport, home had to be close to work. Their chance to move out came therefore with the arrival of industry and cheaper tram transport. Houses were built speculatively, that is, ahead of demand, but this was a risky business with no guarantee of success and development was initially slow. Notice that the estate ended at present-day Exeter Road (then Queens Road). The roads were only extended up to Raddlebarn Road when Raddlebarn Farm was sold in the 1890s.

Opposite above: Junction of Serpentine Road and Oakfield Road, 1962. A good illustration of the 'spacious leafy suburb' of Selly Park, with large houses set in their own grounds. Both the houses in this picture, The Rosary on the left and York House on the right, have since been demolished. A telephone exchange has been built on the former and new houses on the latter.

Opposite below: Building of Selly Wick Housing Association Estate, 1966. The university leased land adjoining Selly Wick House to a housing association, formed by members of staff. In the picture Selly Wick House can be seen on the left and the summerhouse on the right. The bulldozers moved in in 1967. Initially twenty-nine houses were built, grouped around a 'village green' of communal land with each house enjoying a small private garden. Many of the landscape features of Selly Wick House were retained, particularly the mature trees.

Heeley Road, 1905. Heeley Road was formerly a track leading from Raddlebarn Road to Bournbrook Farm (junction of modern-day Exeter and Dawlish Roads). The farm was owned by a gunmaker, John Heeley, who also owned Bournbrook Forge and Mill. The track became a road extending all the way to the Bristol Road just before the development of the estate began in the 1870s. The houses in the picture date from 1870-1900.

Dawlish Road, 1966. This photograph was taken looking along Dawlish Road towards the Bristol Road, with the Goose at the OVT in the background. On the left is Dawlish Road School (now demolished).

Above: Looking towards Hubert Road from Exeter Road in the 1930s. The apparent uniformity of the area conceals great diversity. The houses were built by many independent developers who used different decorative detail on each block of houses. A corner shop at the end of the row of terraces is typical of the estate.

Right: Dawlish Road shop. This was the general store of Emma Gittens at 305 Dawlish Road, run by Emma (in the centre) and her two daughters Alice and Grace. It was noted for its faggots and peas and home-made ice cream. The shop closed down during the Second World War.

Corner shop in Hubert Road, *c.* 1910. Here children pose outside the shop of G.H. Glover, a fish, fruit, rabbit and potato salesman.

Sir John's Road, c. 1910. This development between the Pershore Road and the River Rea in Selly Park was built from 1905 onwards by the firm of Grants Estates. Sir John's Road is named after Sir John Holder, a local brewer and benefactor who lived at Pitmaston, Moor Green Lane. He also owned the Pershore Road Inn (now the Selly Park Tavern). Oliver Floyd of Floyd & Salt was the architect responsible for the houses on this estate and used a wide variety of basic designs, particularly in the front bays and in the ornamentation.

Third Avenue, c. 1910. The estate was built to provide good lower middle class housing for rent, initially 9s 5d, rising to 11s per week by 1917. Typical occupations of the first tenants included a music teacher, an artist, a Baptist minister, a watch repairer and a stonemason. Covenants restricted the building of houses for less than £200 and the land was not to be used for manufacturing or business premises. Note the newly planted trees. The railings on top of the wall were probably removed during the Second World War.

Kitchener Road, pre-1904. In 1899 plans were approved for the building of five new roads, off the Pershore Road – Kitchener, Fashoda, Cecil, Manilla and Hobson Road. These roads were named after late nineteenth century politicians and battles. In the so-called 'Scramble for Africa' Lord Kitchener led the British Army expedition to recapture Fashoda (in the Sudan) from French occupation. Robert Cecil (Marquess of Salisbury) was Conservative Prime Minister for much of the period between 1886 and 1902. Manilla Road may be named after the Battle of Manila, when the Americans destroyed the Spanish Fleet in 1898. The River Rea is at the end of the road, hence the flooding, with Moor Green Woods beyond.

Opposite above: Floods in Sir John's Road, *c.* 1924. The river bed of the Rea was widened and deepened in 1904 but continued to flood. The most serious flood was in 1924 when boats had to be borrowed from Cannon Hill Park to rescue women and children from their homes. The Grants Estates squeezed as many houses as possible onto the site, so flooding would have been an annual problem for many residents. Extensive improvements were made along the river, including culverting large stretches and reinforcing banks.

Opposite below: The River Rea flood in 1999. The River Rea can still rise quickly and flood after heavy downpours. This view is taken further along the Rea near Kitchener Road. Further work was carried out in 2002 to safeguard houses in the area from flooding.

The shop on the corner of Milner Road and St Stephen's/School Road. Milner Road was begun before 1904 and the earliest part of the road to be built was known as Hamilton Road. St Stephen's, or School Road, was so called because it led to St Stephen's Church of England School on Warwards Lane.

Gristhorpe Road, 1915. Permission was given in 1904 for the construction of two new roads off Raddlebarn Road (Umberslade and Gristhorpe Road). These were built across land belonging to the Muntz family whose country home was at Umberslade Hall near Tanworth in Arden. As more and more houses were built in Selly Oak and Bournbrook, anyone seeking to live near the country had to move even further out. One of the first residents of Gristhorpe Road commented that 'living here was like living out in the sticks. We were surrounded by fields'.

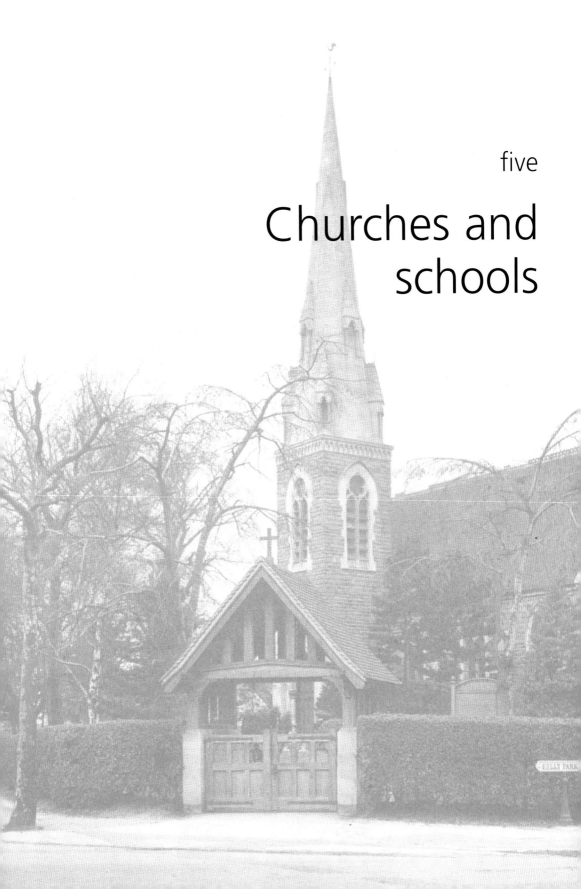

five

Churches and
schools

Above: The first Wesleyan chapel in Selly Oak was built on the Bristol Road in 1835. It was at the right-hand side of the entrance to the Dingle, the small lane which leads down to the Worcester & Birmingham Canal, and opposite to what is now Chapel Lane. A Sunday school was also opened in a room underneath the chapel which gave a general as well as a religious education.

Left: St John's Wesleyan Methodist chapel, which replaced the original chapel, was built on the same site in 1877. It was later enlarged in 1910 and had a school hall. Shown here on a postcard dating from before the First World War, it closed in 1957 when the congregation joined with the Primitive Methodists. A car showroom now occupies the site.

Right: The Primitive Methodist chapel on the north side of the High Street was almost opposite the Wesleyan chapel. The Primitive Methodists first held meetings in 1870 in the open air and in cottages before building a chapel in 1874. This church shown here was rebuilt on the same site in 1907 and was next door to the post office and near to the Birmingham Battery works. After the Methodists Union in 1932 it became St Paul's Methodist Church. In 1957 the two Methodist congregations united, using St Paul's Church until moving to the new Methodist church in Langleys Road in 1966.

Below: This chapel on Raddlebarn Road was opened by the Primitive Methodists in 1901 to serve the expanding population of Bournbrook. This photograph was taken around 1947. The New Apostolic church now occupies a new building on this site.

St Mary's Church, shown here on a postcard of 1906, was built in 1861 using sandstone from a quarry in Weoley Castle. Selly Oak was originally part of the parish of Northfield, and did not have its own parish church until St Mary's was built on land given by J.F. Ledsam, who was then Lord of the Manor.

The bells of St Mary's before recasting in 1932. The ringing master, Mr W.B. Cartwright, is the central figure. The church only contained one bell when it was consecrated, but voluntary subscriptions enabled others to be added until a peal of eight bells was reached in time to honour Queen Victoria's Golden Jubilee in 1887. The bells later became unsafe and had to be recast and rehung.

The original St Mary's School in Selly Oak was first opened as Selly Oak National School in 1860 and was a sandstone building on the corner of Bristol Road and Frederick Road. At that time Selly Oak was expanding rapidly and this school soon became too small, so first a brick infants' school was built adjacent to it and then further schools were built in Dawlish Road and Hubert Road. This school, shown here in a postcard dated 1912, was demolished when the Bristol Road was widened, and a new school was built in Lodge Hill Road.

St Wulstan's Church in Bournbrook (*c.* 1920) originated as a mission hall of St Mary's in 1893 before this church was built in Exeter Road in 1906. The name of St Wulstan was chosen as he was a local saint who was born in Warwickshire and became Bishop of Worcester. This building is now the Elim Pentecostal Church; they exchanged their building in Alton Road with St Wulstan's in 1983 when the parish joined with neighbouring St Stephen's. The Co-op van is outside Ten Acres and Stirchley Co-operative Society (TASCO) Branch No. 1, which was the first purpose-built TASCO branch and opened in 1899.

St Stephen's Church in Serpentine Road was consecrated in 1871 and was at first a chapel of ease of St Mary's but became the separate parish church of St Stephen's, Selly Hill, in 1892. It was built on land given by Robert Dolphin at the top of the hill in the Selly Park estate and the architects were Martin and Chamberlain. The lych gate was added in 1924.

St Stephen's Church hall and Scout hut on the Pershore Road photographed in 1959. The Scout hut was built by the Boy Scouts themselves in around the 1940s. Church services started to be held in the hall from 1977 and it was renamed the Church Centre. It became an additional centre of worship, and finally, in 2004, separated from St Stephen's and became the new parish of Christ Church.

Members of St Stephen's Sunday school around the end of the 1950s, when children wore their school uniform coats and blazers to church on Sundays.

Children from St Stephen's School taking part in the Selly Park Summer Fair organized by St Stephen's Church, c. 1927. Maypole dancing was one of the activities at the fair which was held at a farm by the River Rea on Moor Green Lane.

St Stephen's School in Warwards Lane, *c.* 1918. This was opened as Ten Acres school in 1874. Many community activities were also based here, such as a penny bank and a clothing club. In 1898 a new school building was added to the right-hand side of the original one, which was then used for infants. The site, which was opposite to St Stephen's Road (formerly School Road), was sold in 1966 and the houses in Darris Road built on it.

St Stephen's School infants in Standard 1 in 1920. Edith Lyndon, aged about six, with a bow in her hair, is second from the right on the second row.

Pupils of St Stephen's School in 1910. They appear to be dressed in their Sunday best clothes and many are also wearing flowers as buttonholes or corsages. One of these pupils is Mrs Lily Wright who was then aged fourteen.

The teachers at St Stephen's School in the same year, 1910. Warwards Lane can be seen at the right-hand side of the photograph.

Selly Oak Nursery School in the 1920s. The Nursery School was founded in Greet in 1904, but in 1921 the school moved into premises in Tiverton Road which had been equipped by Mr and Mrs George Cadbury Junior. Many of the children's activities took place on a verandah, open to the air, and in this mealtime photograph, they were supervised by a nurse as well as teachers. In October 1930, a new purpose-built Nursery School was opened on the same site.

Bournbrook School at the bottom of Selly Park Road on the corner with Oakfield Road, as shown in their brochure dated 1912. This was a small Quaker boarding school for twelve boys aged eight to sixteen and contained a lecture room and gymnasium. Although no longer a school, the building was destroyed by a bomb during the Second World War and new houses have now been built on the site.

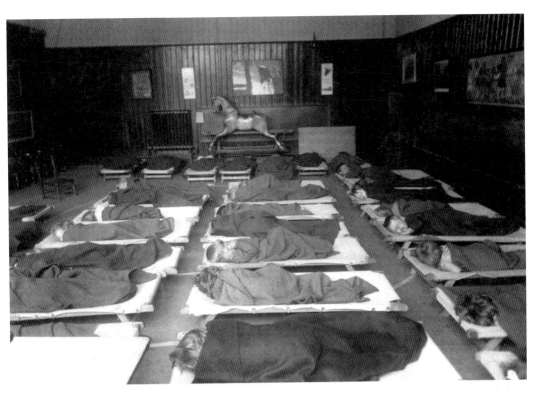

Rest time at Selly Oak Nursery School around 1930, when the school was temporarily relocated to the Mission Hall in Dawlish Road while the new school was being built.

FRIENDS MEETING HOUSE · SELLY OAK · GREEN'S SERIES

This Friends Meeting House on the Bristol Road, almost opposite St Mary's Church, was built about 1927. Previously the Friends had met in the Workman's Hall in Selly Oak and then in the Selly Oak Institute, which was built by George Cadbury in 1894.

Raddlebarn School in 1909 when it had just opened. It replaced the temporary iron buildings which the school had used since its foundation in 1905.

Raddlebarn School infants with dolls and soft toys in 1924. Elsie Faulkner is third from the right on the third row.

Photographs of Tom (aged eight) and Daisy Richards (aged ten) taken at Raddlebarn School to commemorate the Silver Jubilee of King George V in 1935.

A music class for infants at Raddlebarn School around 1932. Tom Richards is seated at the right-hand end of the front row.

Boys from Tiverton Road School, photographed before 1911, after winning a trophy at the Kings Norton Schools Swimming Gala. The school was founded by Kings Norton and Northfield Urban District Council in 1906.

Bournbrook Technical Institute was opened in 1899 to provide a new venue for the evening classes which had been taking place in the manager's house at Elliott's works. In 1896 Elliott's needed to use the house again, so the Local Education Authority built this new Institute on the Bristol Road. This postcard shows that it was also used as an undenominational church. It is now the Oakdale Centre of NACRO (National Association for the Care and Resettlement of Offenders).

Selly Park Baptist Church on the corner of Pershore Road and Selly Park Road was built in 1878. The church had its origins in the Dogpool chapel, a wooden building which was on the corner of St Stephen's Road and Warwards Lane. The Sunday school, which can be seen at the back of the church, was added in 1883. This has now been demolished and a new church built on the site, although the old church still remains.

Selly Park Council School was used as a War Hospital during the First World War. Originally opened in 1911 as a school for all ages, the school is now Selly Park Technology College for Girls.

St Edward's Roman Catholic Church, which is on Raddlebarn Road at the top of Bournbrook Road, was opened in 1902, but soon needed to be enlarged. On this postcard, dated 1905, is written 'I am sending you this postcard so that you can see the Roman Catholic Church which is going to be built on a big hill just at the top of our street... It's not finished yet!'

This aerial photograph of St Paul's Convent shows the chapel and buildings which were added to the existing Selly Hall after the convent was founded in 1864. The old Selly Hall is on the right-hand side facing the chapel. In the background is Selly Park Road and also the prefabs which were built around Selly Park Recreation Ground after the Second World War.

six

Institutions and amenities

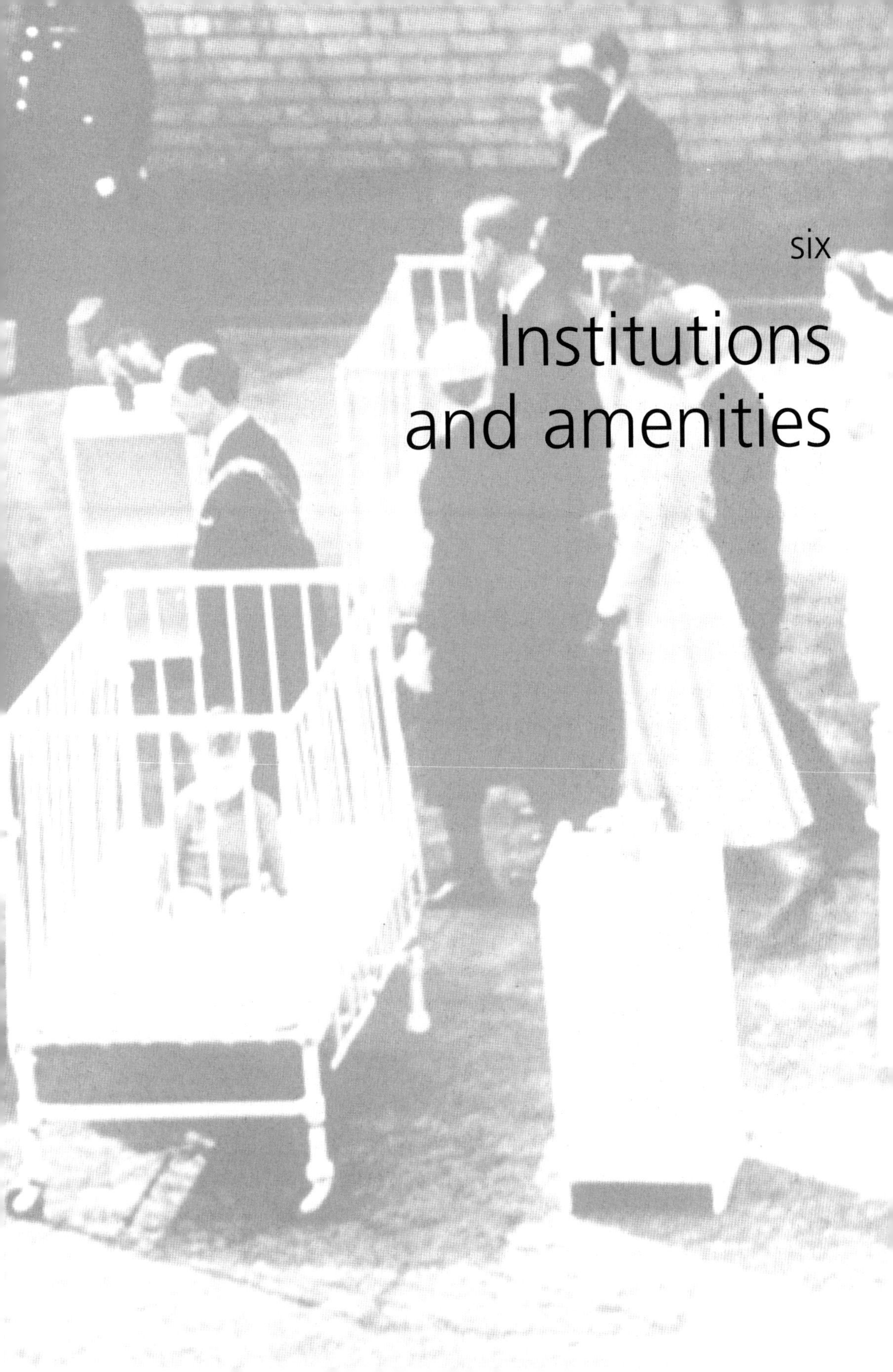

Kings Norton Union Workhouse, pictured in an undated postcard. Selly Oak was part of the Kings Norton Union for Poor Law purposes and in 1872 this workhouse was built in Selly Oak. It was designed by Edward Holmes, the local architect who had designed St Mary's Church. The workhouse cared for the sick as well as the poor and by 1879 housed 400 inmates including 100 'sick and bedridden' and 100 'aged and infirm'. In 1904 casual wards for vagrants and geriatric wards were added to the workhouse. In 1911 the workhouse became part of the Birmingham Union for Poor Law purposes.

A need was recognised to separate workhouses from infirmaries, and in 1895 the foundation stone was laid (on the central twin-gabled building) for a new infirmary, designed by Daniel Arkell. It was built west of the workhouse, separated from it by a wall. In 1906 the infirmary doubled in size, and by the start of the First World War it was known as 'The Hospital'. By 1929, when it housed 550 patients, Birmingham Corporation took it over and Selly Oak became a General Hospital.

Nurses, patients and a doctor in Medical Ward A3, Selly Oak Hospital, Christmas 1934. What appears to be a model fort is displayed. The floor shines to reflect the legs of the hospital beds.

By 1949 the hospital was run under the National Health Service, and a royal visit was arranged when the Children's Ward opened.

These cleaners at Selly Oak Hospital are pictured in 1957 with their cleaning tools. From left to right they are: Mrs Hodgetts, Mrs Catherine (Kate) Richards and Mrs Pryce. Mrs Richards worked in the hospital during the Second World War and lived in Heeley Road.

An aerial view of the hospital taken in the 1920s. The staff playing field and the nurses' home, the Woodlands, are in the foreground. The ex-workhouse buildings are not visible but were on the left (east) of the hospital. As the hospital faced the right-angled turn in Raddlebarn Road the main entrance had to be offset from it.

The Woodlands, the nurses' home, built in 1906 on the other side of Raddlebarn Road to the infirmary.

Guy Dain's house, 1963. In 1902 Harry Guy Dain, who had qualified as a doctor in 1893 in London, was practising from this house on the corner of Bristol Road and Alton Road. In 1947 he is still listed there although the practice is now 'Dain, Haslam and Heath'. Dr Dain was remembered riding a push-bike or visiting in his horse and trap. The church hall of St Stephen's is called the Dain Room after him. By 1969 the medical practice at 480 Bristol Road is 'Heath and Donovan'.

Selly Oak Baths, *c.* 1905. Public Baths were seen as a necessity around 1900 when most houses had little provision for bathing. Selly Oak's baths were built in Tiverton Road in 1905, before Selly Oak was incorporated into Birmingham. The architect was Mr E. Harding Payne and a local building firm, Messrs T.A. Cole & Son, won the tender to build. As well as two swimming pools there were both first and second class private baths, separate ones for men and women. The first superintendents were Mr J. Dunn, a qualified engineer, and his wife, and they had private accommodation on the first floor.

The men's swimming pool shown here had a movable floor fitted over it during the winter which provided a large hall for concerts, political meetings and dances. A smaller, shallower, swimming bath, with steps down into it (deemed advantageous to 'timid bathers') was provided for women and children.

This shows the Selly Oak Fire Brigade in 1905. The 1916 Ordnance Survey map (surveyed in 1882, revised 1914) shows a fire station in The Dingle, the entrance to which led off from Bristol Road opposite Chapel Lane. Pre-1911 the brigade came under Kings Norton and Northfield, and the district was served by stations at Selly Oak and at Kings Heath.

The Infant Welfare Centre, 1922. This was on Harborne Lane and was formerly a public house called 'The Village Bells' (hence the bells at the roof line and etched on the glass). The building shown here was used as a welfare centre where mothers were advised on child care.

The Free Library on Bristol Road before the First World War. The land on which the library was built was donated by Mr Thomas Gibbins Junior, a member of the family which established the Birmingham Battery Company in Selly Oak. He was a local councillor and a county councillor as well as being an industrialist. The philanthropic organisation, the Carnegie Foundation, financed this building as well as other libraries in the area.

Selly Oak Institute, c. 1905. Built by George Cadbury in 1894 and originally serving as a meeting place for the Society of Friends, the Institute also provided a recreational centre for the locality and for the Severn Street School. The latter was in central Birmingham and provided adult education classes out of work hours. Various clubs met in the Institute as did a choir and a band. In 1937 it was the address for the relieving officer and the registrar of births, marriages and deaths, as well as a Men's Social Club, a Girls' Gymnastic club, Selly Oak Choral Union and a dancing teacher, Miss Christine Boyse.

Selly Park post office, pictured here in 1923, was at 580 Pershore Road adjacent to Sir John's Road. From at least 1917 until 1947 Edmund Colin Gilbert was running the post office and a grocery. He lived at 582, on the opposite corner of Sir John's Road. In the 1920s Edward J. Grizzells' Pershore Road Garage was next door to the post office at 578 Pershore Road.

The police station in 1963. Situated on the corner of Oak Tree Lane and Bristol Road, this purpose-built police station – which housed a superintendent – replaced an earlier house, which, along with the adjoining property, was used in the days before 1911 and the incorporation of Selly Oak into Birmingham. There was also a (Worcestershire) County Police Station at 58 Alton Road in 1907 manned by Constable Frederick Roberts.

Selly Oak was the base for a complex of colleges which began when George Cadbury opened a study centre for the Society of Friends at his old house, Woodbrooke, in 1903. The colleges catered for a variety of religious affiliations, and training missionaries was an important part of their work. The College of the Ascension was founded in 1923 by the United Society for the Propagation of the Gospel, which converted two houses on Bristol Road. By 1930 the college was no longer large enough and it moved to new premises, leaving the original college free to be taken over by the Church of Christ as a theological college, called Overdale.

The University of Birmingham, pictured in an undated postcard. Situated in Edgbaston, the main gate to the university is on Bristol Road opposite Bournbrook Road and just across the Bourn Brook border of Selly Oak. The university has had a major impact on Selly Oak since construction began on the site in 1901. Erection of the superstructure of the Great Hall, larger than Birmingham's Town Hall, began in 1905. King Edward VII formally opened the university on 7 July 1909 in a ceremony in the Great Hall. The university still holds its degree congregations there.

The University of Birmingham, again from an undated postcard. When the First World War began
in 1914 the completed university buildings were taken over as the First Southern General Military
Hospital, providing 540 beds, soon expanded to 1,000. Casualties were brought here by ambulances
after arrival by train at Selly Oak goods yard. When the university resumed its educational
function, Selly Oak and Bournbrook provided lodgings for students and homes for staff.

Muntz Park was originally a small recreation ground of 5 acres, created in 1905 when Mr F.E.
Muntz donated land between Umberslade and Gristhorpe Roads. He sold the council further
land in 1907 and 1909 to extend the park. The Muntz family, of Muntz Metals, had owned land in
Selly Oak from the 1840s. In 1925 a stage, dressing rooms and bandstand were built in Muntz Park
giving facilities for public entertainment and dances in the part called 'The Dell'.

Evans Cottage Homes, for 'ladies of reduced fortunes', were endowed and built in 1868 by Alfred Smith Evans at 863 to 867 Bristol Road, near to its junction with Lodge Hill Road. The Post Office Directory of Worcestershire for 1876 describes them as a 'tasteful group of buildings consisting of nine dwellings'. Alfred Smith Evans lived in Westbourne Road, Edgbaston, at a house called Mariemont.

Lodge Hill Cemetery, 1910. The Rural Sanitary Authority bought the site of Lodge Hill Cemetery for £3,528 and the buildings cost a further £5,000. The fact that Kings Norton Union had given notice that there was no further accommodation for burial of the workhouse inmates brought a sense of urgency. The cemetery was consecrated in 1896 by the Bishop of Coventry. In 1937 Birmingham's municipal crematorium was built here, designed by Holland W. Hobbiss, the Arts and Crafts architect.

seven

Pubs,
cinemas,
sports and
community

The Malt Shovel Inn (1860s) was the predecessor of the current Goose at the OVT. This was also the site of Selly Oak's Victorian fun park – Kirby's Pools. It was described in 1885 as 'A well-known and favourite resort on the outskirts of the borough, on the Bristol Road and formerly one of the celebrated taverns and tea gardens of past days'. The Pools, which had been mill pools for a forge on the Bourn Brook, were named after the Malt Shovel's landlord around 1820-59, James Kirby. In 1860 George North took over as licensed victualler with George James, maltster, as his partner. Just a three-mile walk or a brief tram ride away, Kirby's Pools were a big draw to the workers of Birmingham, seeking recreation, and perhaps some fishing, in fresh country air.

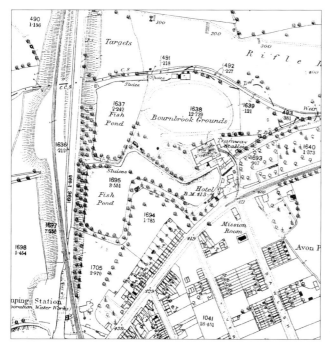

Around 1876 the Malt Shovel and its grounds were acquired by the Bournbrook Hotel and Garden Company. The Bournbrook Hotel ('Hotel' in centre of 1890 map) was built to replace the Malt Shovel. That name is in stone on the face of the building. The grounds were laid out, and a grand ornamental entrance was made with a turnstile ('Bournbrook Grounds' on the upper part of the map). Spectacles were staged here including firework displays and balloon ascents. In 1878 a cricket match against a visiting Australian team attracted a gate on the first of the three days of play of 12,000. The 1890s saw local attractions losing ground as cheap rail travel opened up new horizons and the Pools were filled in and housing and factories built over them.

The Gun Barrels Inn (undated photograph) is just over the border in Edgbaston. An earlier building sits behind the one appearing here and it could be that marked 'The Grinders' on an 1819 turnpike map. There was a gun barrel manufactory belonging to William Deakin at Bournbrook in 1841, and the Gun Barrels' name probably originates from that trade.

The Gun Barrels, from a postcard marked 1907. Like many rural inns, the Gun Barrels had an adjacent bowling green. This shows the older building at right angles to the one facing Bristol Road.

The Selly Park Tavern, Pershore Road, in an undated photograph. This was built in 1901 as the Selly Park Hotel, in the Arts and Crafts style for Holders Brewery, replacing the Pershore Inn, which probably dated back to the building of Pershore Road in 1825. Sir John Charles Holder, the founder of Holder's Brewery, lived in Moseley, and his initials appear in the middle gable. From 1920 Mitchells and Butlers absorbed Holders Brewery. The tavern has a separate skittle alley, probably one of the earlier inn's outbuildings.

The Dogpool Inn, Pershore Road, *c.* 1915. It appears as an inn on an 1877 map. The chimney of Dogpool Mill is in the distance. The sign writers' craft is well displayed here, detailing the beverages available from the landlord, Tom G.H. Thompson.

The Dog and Partridge, Bristol Road, in an undated photograph. Behind the façade was an old farmhouse which had sold its home-brewed beer from the early days of Selly Oak's canalside development. It had been run by an independent beer retailer until 1938 when Mitchells and Butlers bought it. The Dog and Partridge survived until the 1990s, when it was demolished.

When this photograph was taken in the late 1960s the pub was the Station Inn, but it is situated at the junction of Bristol Road and Heeley Road and began as The Heeley Arms. In the 1881 census the publican was twenty-seven-year-old Thomas Thompson, born in Bath, who lived there with his wife Elizabeth and their two young children, John and Alice, and a fifteen-year-old servant, Sarah Sharratt. This pub has now been renamed the Bristol Pear.

The Oak Inn, 1950. This pub is situated on Bristol Road at its junction with Harborne Lane. It faced across Bristol Road to the site of the old oak tree. Early photographs show a horse drinking trough outside. The Oak was demolished in the prelude to the redevelopment of the triangle site currently occupied by a Sainsbury's store.

The Plough and Harrow in an undated photograph. Also on Bristol Road, on the corner with Chapel Lane, this pub was originally the New Inn, but changed to the Plough and Harrow in 1904. The squirrel motif of Holt's Brewery can be seen on the gable. That brewery was founded in 1887 in Aston, but was taken over by Ansell's Brewery Ltd in 1934. Across the road some way further along is the distinctive flat-roofed profile of the Dog and Partridge.

The White Horse was on Chapel Lane and remained a beer house until 1957 when it got a full license. In the 1990s it fell victim to the redevelopment of the triangle currently occupied by a Sainsbury's store.

The Country Girl pub on Raddlebarn Road provides a contrast to the more urban style of the White Horse. The garden at the back is now a car park, but in the years before the First World War, when this photograph was taken, it had a pleasant rural feel with its beer garden laid out with tables and benches. In 1881 it is listed as a beer house.

Above: This pub on Pershore Road on the corner of St Stephen's Road replaced an earlier inn called the Ten Acres Inn. It faced another old inn, the Dogpool Inn, which sat diagonally across from it on Dogpool Lane. When both of the old inns were demolished, the Dogpool name transferred to this fine building, which has its original name, 'The Dogpool Hotel' carved into its stonework, along with the name of the brewery, Holt's, which built the pub. It is currently called the Hibernian.

Left: 'The Steps' or Bournbrook Tavern, possibly in the 1950s. Another Bournbrook pub, this Mitchells & Butlers house was officially called the Bournbrook Tavern, but was commonly referred to as the Steps. The flight of steps up to its front door are being used by the group posing for the photographer.

The Picturedrome sat at the north side of Chapel Lane next to the Plough and Harrow. St Mary's church hall, the People's Hall, was also used to screen cinema shows in the early days, as was a small picture house called the Bournbrook Electric Theatre in Grange Road. When the large cinema called the Oak opened in 1924, the Picturedrome became a billiard hall, and later was used as a factory.

The Oak cinema. The 1920s saw the rapid rise of cinema as popular entertainment and grandiose super-sized cinemas succeeded the smaller more improvised picture houses. Built on the opposite corner of Chapel Lane to the Picturedrome, the Oak was seen as representing cutting-edge cinema design when it opened its doors in 1924, meriting an article in the *Architects' Journal*.

The interior of the Oak cinema, 1924. At its maximum the Oak could seat 1,500 people, although it was originally built for 900 in the auditorium and 300 on the balcony. This interior view, from the *Architects' Journal*, shows its original layout.

This is the classically inspired frieze that would have greeted patrons in the foyer. The luxurious ambience and the lively entertainment would have provided some escape from the harsh reality of the Depression which blighted the 1920s and 1930s. The cinema closed in 1979.

Opposite above: Selly Park Football Club, *c.* 1932. This photograph is of the club commemorating their winning of the North Birmingham Cup in 1931/32. The players' names have been added. F. Huskisson (fifth from the left in the back row) lived in Tiverton Road and was one of a family of ten children.

Opposite below: A picture of ladies playing croquet in the 1920s. The venue might be adjacent to the Gun Barrels Inn, on the Bristol Road.

WRIGHT WILSON BELL PIRSON THOMAS ARCHER BOWIN LEWIS FENBY PARKES
HUSKISON BRANDON (Sec) (Chairman)

BRADLEY GRENDON. BRADLEY KEMISH VICKERY NADDON. MILLER
(Trainer)

SELLY PARK F.C
WINNERS
NORTH BIRMINGHAM
CUP
1931-32

Celebrations in 1945. At the end of the Second World War parties were held all over Britain to celebrate the ending of hostilities in the two theatres of war: Europe (VE Day) and Japan (VJ Day). This children's party was held in the Methodist Hall, Pershore Road, to celebrate one of those events. Rationing was still in force, so it is likely that the food would not have run to many luxuries.

Street party in Heeley Road, 1945. The tables and chairs are out in the road for this party in Heeley Road, celebrating Victory in Europe, which came on 8 May 1945. There appear to have been many young families living in Heeley Road then. Although nearby Hubert and Dawlish Road sustained bomb damage during the war, Heeley Road survived unscathed.

Coronation celebrations in Kitchener Road 1953. After VJ Day, the next occasion for big street parties was the Coronation of the young Queen Elizabeth II on 2 June 1953. The bunting is out in Kitchener Road and the residents pose for a souvenir photograph (to go with the Coronation mugs and spoons that were distributed to schoolchildren to mark the event).

Church outing, 1955. The ladies are about to embark on a St Stephen's Church coach outing in 1955 and pose in Pershore Road wearing their best hats and coats.

During the 1970s Selly Oak held successful annual festivals, which involved processions of floats and entertainment to suit all ages. There were concerts, Asian and Irish dancing, tug-of-war contests and children's skateboarding competitions, as well as five-a-side football.

Selly Oak Festival, 1970s. These children sit on top of the cab of their float during the festival. It was during the 1970s that the wearing of car seatbelts became compulsory, but those sitting on vehicles' roofs were exempt!

eight

Up and down the Bristol Road

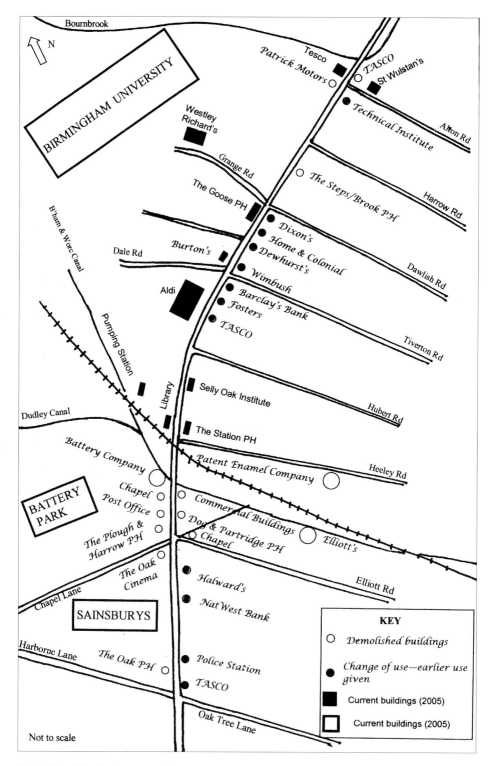

Bristol Road landmarks, past and present.

Bristol Road, 1925. This view is looking towards Bournbrook, with Edgbaston Park Road on the right and the old Gun Barrels pub beyond. The Bristol Road appears on a map of 1369 and has been an important route ever since, although not following the same alignment. The current line of the road out of Birmingham to this point was not constructed until 1771. Before that the road into Birmingham went by way of Edgbaston Park Road (which then began opposite Bournbrook Road), alongside Edgbaston Park (now Edgbaston Golf Course), along Priory Road, Church Road, Arthur Road, Wheeley's Road, Bath Row, Holloway Head and Smallbrook Ringway. A new section of turnpike was made in 1771 at a cost of £5,000, starting at Bristol Street and joining the older road near the Gun Barrels and that part of the old road across Edgbaston Park was abandoned. The boundary between Edgbaston and Selly Oak starts where the Bourn Brook crosses the Bristol Road.

Co-op, Bournbrook. This fine building was Branch No. 9 of the Ten Acres and Stirchley Co-operative Society (TASCO) and stood on the corner of the Bristol Road and Alton Road. It opened in 1908 to cater for the university community, but it was not a success and was known as the Society's only 'white elephant'. It closed as a branch of TASCO in the 1960s. The building was used for a while by Lewis, Woolf & Griptight but was demolished in the 1970s. The site is now occupied by HSS Equipment Hire.

Patrick Motors, 1963. This is currently the site of Tesco Express, which is itself likely to be demolished to make way for the new link road.

Bournbrook, 1929. This view is taken looking south along the Bristol Road with Harrow Road on the left. The shop on the corner, with the awnings, is Westwoods, greengrocers. Note the houses on the right still have small enclosed front gardens.

A close-up of the same corner in 1963. The shop next to Westwood's was a pharmacy, 'Pharos', and is still a chemist's. This corner block of six shops with residences above (described as 'three-storey retail shops' in the planning application) was built in 1896 – one of the first developments of the Selly Grove Estate which encompassed Alton, Harrow, Luton, Croydon and Arley Roads.

Bristol Road (north side) in Bournbrook, 1963. The Bristol Road in Bournbrook and Selly Oak was a shopping street from the early twentieth century, with a peak period of growth between 1900 and 1950. This view is taken looking towards its junction with Grange Road. Note the National Provincial Bank – one of three banks on the Bristol Road in Selly Oak and Bournbrook in 1969.

Beatrix Gown Manufacturers at 521 Bristol Road, photographed in 1963. This was one of several clothing outlets on the Bristol Road. Many of the ladies' clothes shops along the Bristol Road in the 1960s had women's names such as 'Kitty's', 'Molly's' and 'Lilian's'.

High Street, Bournbrook, from an undated postcard.

Bristol Road in Bournbrook. This view is taken looking north towards Birmingham, with Grange Road in the foreground on the left. The three-storey public house the Bournbrook Tavern (also called 'The Steps' and later 'The Brook') can just be seen on the right behind the elaborate wrought-iron lamp-post.

Dawlish Road corner, 1963. The corner premises of Alfred Shield Ltd, pawnbrokers. The shop next door was that of Thomas Clarke, a fruiterer. The site has been occupied for a number of years by the Phoenix Café. There is a plaque with the description 'Market Place' on this building.

Bristol Road, 1963. This block of shops includes Dewhurst's, a chain of butchers which was one of the first multiples to arrive in Bournbrook in the late 1940s, marking the beginnings of a trend away from the smaller, sole owner outlet towards the larger, more impersonal multiples. Also in this block is the 'Home and Colonial' general provisions store. Next door to this shop was Dixon's, described in 1937 as a 'ladies outfitters'.

Where can I get it?

How often have you asked yourself this question? You may have wanted a good confectioner, a smart ladies' outfitter, a reliable chemist, a high-class grocer or butcher . . . and a hundred other things. A look through the advertisements in this magazine may help you to solve your question.

ALSO AT
108-110 LOZELLS ROAD, ASTON.

549 BEARWOOD ROAD, SMETHWICK.

24 CAPE HILL, SMETHWICK.
and
"LADIESWEAR"
1132 STRATFORD ROAD, HALL GREEN.

Agents for
"SWALLOW"
Raincoats.

For everything in
LADIES' WEAR
try . . .

DIXON'S

It is Their pleasure to serve You well - Their endeavor to give You that EXTRA VALUE and PERSONAL ATTENTION that a suburban shop should do.

572-574 Bristol Road, Bournbrook.

Left: Advertisement for Dixon's, 1938. This appeared in the parish magazine of St Stephen's, Selly Hill in 1938. Dixon's was described by one older resident as 'Posh! Double fronted with a wall round. They sold hats upstairs. Very select and pricey!'

Below: Burton's, 1963. A familiar landmark in Bournbrook for many years, Burton's opened in the 1940s. The site is now in use as a stationer's.

High Street, Bournbrook, *c.* 1900. A bustling suburban shopping street, with the Bournbrook Hotel in the background. The corner later occupied by Burton's has an even older shop on the site.

Corner of Tiverton Road. A similar view in 1963. A.D. Wimbush was established as a confectioner in Bournbrook by 1917 and by 1947 Wimbush was trading as a chain of bakers. This corner plot is now occupied by a student travel company.

Bristol Road, 1963. A typical view of Bournbrook – a row of varied shops to meet the needs of suburban dwellers. Foster Brothers was one of several tailors on the High Street, offering ready-made suits as well as a 'tailoring to measure' service. Also included in this block of shops is a branch of TASCO which also produced its own goods, as well as running a bakery, a dairy and, here in this row, a butcher's. On the far left of the row is a branch of Barclays Bank.

High Street, Bournbrook, 1904.

Bristol Road, 1937. This view is taken looking down the Bristol Road towards the railway bridge. All the buildings on the right of the picture have now been demolished.

Bristol Road, 1992. These buildings, known as the 'Commercial Buildings', were erected in 1903. Although renovated in 1986, they were eventually demolished in 1992. To the right of the picture can be seen the Primitive Methodist chapel and the post office, now the site of Halfords.

A view taken of the junction with Chapel Lane in 1913. On the right is the Plough and Harrow public house. The houses opposite the Plough and Harrow (on the same side) were later demolished to make way for the Oak cinema and later for Sainsbury's. The pedestrians on the left of the picture are walking past St John's Methodist Church.

Bristol Road, 1959. This view is taken looking from the junction with Chapel Lane towards the junction with Oak Tree Lane. The Oak public house can be seen in the distance on the right of the picture. All the properties before the Oak were demolished to make way for Sainsbury's in the early 1980s.

Left: Halward's butcher's shop. Halward's was a pork butcher's shop, established in 1892 by Thomas Halward. Ownership passed down the family until Alfred Halward's retirement in 1973. The shop was located close to the old police station.

Below: Selly Oak Fishmonger's. In 1928 this fishmonger's had been replaced by William Edward Reynolds, a furniture broker. The firm continued until the 1970s and was located at 736 Bristol Road.

Junction with Harborne Lane, 1963. The former narrow turning from the Bristol Road onto Harborne Lane. The Oak public house is on the far side of the junction. The houses on the left of the picture were all demolished to make way for road widening.

Leaving Selly Oak, 1938. The view in this postcard is taken by the junction with Weoley Park Road and looks along the Bristol Road towards Northfield.

Other local titles published by Tempus

Birmingham: The Building of a City

JOSEPH MCKENNA

Since the time of William Hutton's history of Birmingham in 1780, there has been no real attempt to describe and explain the physical growth of Birmingham as a city and to consider its development. When was the growth and why did it occur? What created the city street plans we see today? Who were the men who designed, financed and built modern Birmingham? This fascinating book provides answers to these important questions and more.

0 7524 3489 6

Birmingham Cinemas

CHRISTINE WILKINSON AND MARGARET HANSON

Through the medium of old photographs, advertisements and programmes, this book provides a fascinating look at the history of cinema-going in the city of Birmingham, from its early beginning as a fairground attraction right up to the present day and the giant multiplex cinema. This comprehensive volume is sure to appeal to those who remember visiting some of the now long-gone movie houses and anyone else with an interest in the architectural and social history of Birmingham.

0 7524 3080 7

Catholics in Birmingham

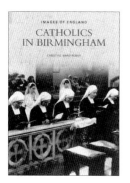

CHRISTINE WARD-PENNY

The growth of the Catholic community in Birmingham during the nineteenth and twentieth centuries is a remarkable story. In 1786 there were fewer than 500 Catholics in the city, yet by 1841 there were sufficient number to warrant the building of St Chad's Cathedral. With almost 200 photographs, many from the archives of Birmingham Central Library, this book captures the flavour of what Roman Catholics have brought to Birmingham and this book is dedicated to their history and tradition.

0 7524 3362 8

Central Birmingham 1950-1980

MARTIN HAMPSON

This collection of over 200 photographs, drawn from the archives held at Birmingham Central Library, recalls a bygone age when trams trundled down Victorian streets and steam trains halted at soot-blackened stations. The years immediately following the Second World War were more changeable than most, partly because the war itself delayed many plans for the city, and partly because of the need for post-war reconstruction.

0-7524-3361-X

If you are interested in purchasing other books published by Tempus, or in case you have difficulty finding any Tempus books in your local bookshop, you can also place orders directly through our website

www.tempus-publishing.com